Nature's Children

LEOPARDS

Sheila Dalton

Grolier

FACTS IN BRIEF

Classification of the Leopard

Class: *Mammalia* (mammals)
Order: *Carnivora* (meat-eaters)
Family: *Felidae* (cat family)
Genus: *Panthera*
Species: *Panthera pardus* (leopard)

World distribution.   Southern Africa, Southern Asia; scattered populations in northern Africa, Arabia, the Far East.

Habitat.   Can live in almost any habitat as long as there is enough food and water and a certain amount of cover from which to hunt.

Distinctive physical characteristics.   Most have black spots arranged in rosettes on a tawny background. Whiskers are very developed for hunting at night; long, thick tail.

Habits.   Basically solitary. Hunts mainly at night.

Diet.   Small animals and the young of larger species, birds, insects and fish.

Published originally as
"Getting to Know . . . Nature's Children."

This series is approved and recommended by the Federation of Ontario Naturalists.

This library reinforced edition is available exclusively from:

Grolier Educational Corporation
Sherman Turnpike, Danbury, Connecticut 06816

Copyright © 1990 by Grolier Limited. All rights reserved.
Printed and Bound in U.S.A.   ISBN 0-7172-2640-9

Contents

Everyone is fascinated by leopards. Their mixture of strength and beauty is so striking that they have inspired countless folk tales. They have also been used by many organizations as a symbol for power and grace.

In West Africa about 200 years ago, people so admired the leopard's strength that even its whiskers were thought to have special powers. It was said that, chopped up and sprinkled in an enemy's food, they were sure to make the enemy sicken and die!

What is it about leopards that makes them both feared and admired? Let's take a closer look at these powerful, secretive animals.

Leopard Land

The leopard is the most widespread cat in the world. That's partly because it isn't a picky eater. A leopard will eat just about anything it comes across, so it doesn't need to stick close to any one type of animal or habitat.

Leopards are found in Africa, the Middle East and southern Asia. They are equally at home in tropical forests, open grasslands, semideserts and even on mountainsides. They can survive in very hot and very cold climates. As long as there is water to drink and enough cover so they can stalk their prey unseen, leopards are happy.

*The colored areas
on this map show
where leopards
live.*

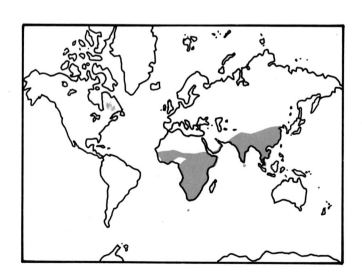

The Cat Family

The leopard is a member of the cat family. It has sharp claws, long whiskers and a fur coat just like a house cat. But the leopard can do something a house cat can't do—roar. The small cats, which include bobcats, lynx, cougars and house cats, cannot roar but they can purr. Lions, tigers, jaguars and leopards are known as big cats. They can roar, but they cannot purr—at least not continuously the way your pet cat can. Some of them can make purring sounds, but they have to stop to breathe.

Although there are several cats that are called leopards there is only one real leopard. The rare clouded leopard and the snow leopard, or ounce, are both distinct species from the leopard.

The snow leopard lives in the mountainous and forested regions of Asia.

Seeing Spots

The leopard's coat is spotted for a good reason. It makes it very difficult to see. Whether lying in long grass, in forest undergrowth or high up in a tree, its coat blends in perfectly with the patterns of light and shade around it. This helps make the leopard a good hunter. It can creep up very close to its prey without being seen.

A leopard is usually tawny yellow with blackish brown spots. On most of its body, the spots are arranged in rosettes. Rosettes are small circles made up of spots. The jaguar, the leopard's larger American cousin, has a very similar coat, but it is not quite the same. The difference is that the rosettes on a jaguar usually have one or more spots in the center, whereas those on the leopard hardly ever do.

The leopard has small spots on its head and larger ones on its body.

Spotless

There is one type of leopard that doesn't appear to have any spots at all. This leopard is sometimes called a "black panther" because its coat is so dark. But it isn't really black, it's a very dark shade of brown. And it does have spots. They are almost the same color as its background fur, however, and can only be seen when the animal is in bright sunlight.

The dark leopard is mainly found in moist, dense forests in Asia. It is quite rare. Although dark and tawny cubs may be born in the same litter, both parents must be dark in order to produce all dark cubs.

Can you spot the spots on this dark leopard's coat?

Mighty Cat

The leopard is the smallest member of the big cat family but it is very strong. A leopard weighs between 30 and 90 kilograms (66 to 198 pounds). That's less than half the size of a tiger. But a leopard has such powerful legs and jaws that it can carry its prey up into trees. That's pretty remarkable when the prey is a young zebra or antelope—animals that weigh at least as much as the leopard itself!

Leopards range in size from just under a metre to almost 2 metres (3 to 7 feet) in length. And that doesn't include their tail. Males are usually twice the size of females.

The leopard is an agile and graceful climber.

Tale of a Tail

A leopard's tail is thick and long—almost as long as its body, in fact. And it is very useful.

A mother leopard strokes her cubs with her tail. She also encourages them to play by waving it in front of them. When she tires of the game, she springs high up into a tree where the cubs cannot reach her. Her tail comes in handy there, too. It helps her to balance on branches with the ease of a tightrope walker.

The underside of a leopard's tail is usually white. As a mother leopard moves ahead of her young through thick undergrowth, she loops her tail up over her back, where it is easy for the cubs to see and follow.

A leopard's tail may grow to be a metre (3 feet) long.

Not Just a Cuddly Cat

Like the other big cats the leopard
has long sharp claws. These come in
handy for climbing trees and for
hunting. When running the leopard
retracts, or pulls its claws into its
paws, to keep them sharp. This also
helps it to approach its prey silently.
When it is ready to spring the
leopard extends its claws.

Along with its claws the leopard's
long, pointed canine teeth help it to
hold and kill its prey. The back
teeth cut up the leopard's food into
bite-sized pieces so it can be
swallowed. And its rough tongue,
which is covered in tiny hooks, is
perfect for cleaning the last bits of
meat off bones.

*The soft pads on its feet and the
fur between its toes help the
leopard to walk quietly.*

20

Leaping Leopards

The leopard is one of the super athletes of the animal kingdom. Although it usually moves slowly and silently, it can run up to 60 kilometres (40 miles) per hour when it needs to. That's faster than a car driving down a city street! No wonder the leopard can run at its top speed only in short spurts.

Leopards are also champion broad jumpers, able to cover more than 6 metres (20 feet) in a single bound. Even more amazingly, they can leap half that far straight up in the air. That's as high as a basketball hoop! And not only is the leopard the best tree climber in the big cat family, it is also a strong swimmer.

Keeping watch.

Leopard Language

Although leopards are not noisy animals, they can roar, grunt and make purring sounds. Their roar is more like a rasping cough than a mighty bellow, and the leopard uses it to contact other leopards, mostly at mating time. A male will also roar to let other males know they've entered his territory.

Zoologists observing leopards in the wild have noted at least two other leopard sounds: chuffling and chirping. Chuffling is a sound made by blowing air sharply through the nostrils. One zoologist heard a mother leopard chuffle to call her cubs. Another heard a leopard make an odd, high-pitched chirping noise whenever she was afraid for her cubs' safety.

Panting helps the leopard to cool off on a hot day.

Body Language

On the back of each of its rounded ears, the leopard has a white spot set against a black background. These spots, as well as the white underside of the leopard's tail, help cubs keep track of their mother when they are following her through thick underbrush. But why do males have them too when they hardly ever help care for the cubs? Some zoologists think that when leopards meet to mate, and on those rare occasions when they hunt together, they flick their ears a certain way to send messages. "Come on over," "Go away," or "This way to the food!" may all be signaled by ear movements.

Notice the white spot on the back of this leopard's ear.

Hide and Seek

Even now, we know more about lions, tigers and jaguars than we do about leopards. This is because leopards are very secretive. They are active mainly at night and their senses are specially suited for getting around in the dark.

In daylight, leopards probably see no better than you do, but a special reflective material in their eyes gives them excellent night vision. Their long whiskers help them at night too, by acting as feelers that warn them of branches and anything else in their path. Leopards also have a keen sense of smell and cup-shaped ears that move to pinpoint exactly where a sound is coming from. With their sensitive nose and exceptional hearing they can easily avoid people and can locate prey even if they can't see it. This is particularly useful when traveling through forests and dense vegetation.

Leopards almost always hunt alone.

Food, Glorious Food

The leopard is a carnivore, or meat eater. It feeds on just about anything that moves—from tiny beetles to young giraffes. Although a leopard mainly eats impala, other gazelles and wildebeest it will also dine on frogs, lizards, birds, monkeys, rats, pigs and baboons. It may supplement its meaty diet with grass, eggs and fruit.

Leopards have a taste for fish as well. They sometimes lie on the banks of rivers or lakes, flipping large fish out of the water with their paws.

A young leopard practices its stalking skills on a lizard.

Hunting Habits

Leopards usually hunt at night. Often they stalk their prey silently, slinking along with their belly close to the ground, before dashing forward and pouncing. Unsuspecting smaller prey are sometimes killed when they are resting without any chase at all. A leopard may also drop down from a tree branch onto prey passing below. It can hunt while in a tree, too, giving chase to the monkeys and birds that live there.

A leopard strangles its prey by grabbing it by the throat, or kills it with a bite to the back of the neck. Then it carries its prey high into the branches of a tree, beyond the reach of other meat-eaters, such as lions and wild dogs. If the animal is too large to eat all at once, the leopard will come back to feed day after day until there is nothing left. It doesn't care if the meat is rotten.

Pity the poor animal that comes strolling under this tree!

Private Property

Leopards live and hunt within an area known as their home range. The size of the range varies. Ten square kilometres (4 square miles) is plenty if there's lots of food and water. If either is in short supply, 40 square kilometres (16 square miles) might not be big enough.

Females often have overlapping ranges, but males refuse to share with each other. A male leopard warns other males off his territory by scratching trees and digging holes. He even sprays urine on trees to leave a scent that tells other males to keep out. If they're foolish enough not to take the hint, a fight will result. Luckily, the scents and signals are usually enough to send an unwanted visitor packing.

Sometimes it's very tiring being a leopard.

Getting Together

For most of the year, leopards live alone. They even avoid each other's company. A male and female usually get together only to mate, then separate again after a few days. Though cases have been noted where the male helps raise the young by bringing food to them, this is far from common.

Mating takes place at any time of the year and cubs can be born in any season. The female attracts the male with a combination of smells and sounds. She travels far and wide, leaving scent markings for the male to follow or calling quietly with a special mating call. After mating she usually chases the male away.

The happy couple.

Cuddly Cubs

About three months after mating, the female leopard gives birth. She can have anywhere from one to six cubs, but usually has two or three.

The newborn leopards are quite small, weighing only about 450 grams (a pound), not much more than a young kitten. They are covered with dull gray fur that shows just a hint of spots, but their eyes are tightly shut and they are completely helpless.

It will be about a week or ten days before the cubs open glazed bluish eyes to get their first look at the world. Meanwhile they spend their time sleeping and nursing on their mother's rich milk.

You can tell that this cub is several weeks old by its clear blue eyes and its well-defined spots.

Early Days

The mother leopard hides her babies in a rock crevice or a hollow tree and usually transfers them to a new hiding place every few days. This makes it much harder for a hungry jackal, hyena or eagle to find them.

Mother and cubs enjoy being close to each other. The mother grooms her cubs often, and they greet each other by rubbing their faces or bodies together. When the cubs are a little older, they tumble and play fight at every opportunity.

You'd have to be very brave or very foolish—and probably both—to try to get near this mother's cub.

Growing Up

At first, the helpless cubs are guarded day and night by their mother. She leaves only when she has to hunt for food. While she is gone, the cubs never venture from the den, no matter how hungry they become.

When they are first allowed out under mother's watchful eye, they spend their time crouching motionless, camouflaged amongst the shadows. Soon, however, the cubs venture farther afield. They are the most vulnerable when they're not yet familiar with their surroundings. Small and weak, they are in danger of attack from predators. Fortunately their mother is devoted and tries to protect them from all intruders.

It's not long before a young leopard cub is following its mother everywhere.

Leopard Lessons

When they are four to six months old, the young cubs begin to accompany their mother on hunting trips. She teaches them how to hide from enemies and how to stalk and catch prey. These are not easy skills to acquire and the learning process can be dangerous. Sometimes prey will fight back, and a desperate baboon or wild pig may prove too much for a young cub to handle. Cubs are often hurt and sometimes killed. It could take almost two years before they are ready to hunt on their own.

All senses alert.

Leaving Home

The leopard cubs stay close to their mother until they are at least a year old. After that, they start to spend time on their own, gradually becoming more and more independent. By the time they are about two, the mother is ready to give birth to a new litter, and the youngsters must leave and fend for themselves.

The males set out to establish their own territory. Females usually take over part of their mother's range, though they rarely spend time with her. If they have learned their lessons well, the young leopards can expect to live about ten more years and have several families of their own.

Words to Know

Camouflage   Colors and patterns that help an animal blend in with its surroundings.

Canine tooth   One of four strong pointed teeth, located between the front teeth and the molars.

Carnivore   Literally, ''meat eater.'' A mammal that feeds mainly on flesh.

Chuffling   A sound made by blowing air sharply through the nostrils.

Cub   A young leopard.

Habitat   The area or type of area in which an animal or plant naturally lives.

Home range   Area where an animal lives and hunts.

Predator   An animal that hunts other animals for food.

Prey   An animal hunted or killed by another animal for food.

Retract   Draw back into the body.

Rosette   A small circle made up of spots.

Territory   Area that an animal or group of animals lives in and often defends from other animals of the same kind.

Wildebeest   Large African antelope, also called gnu.

Zoologist   Scientist who studies animals.

INDEX

Cover Photo: Bill Ivy

Photo Credits: Bill Ivy, pages 4, 8, 12, 16-17, 21, 25, 26, 34; Peter Arnold / Hot Shots, page 7; Cynthia and Amor Klotzbach, page 11; G.C. Kelley, pages 15, 18; Superstock / Four By Five, pages 22, 33; Len Rue Jr., page 29; Breck Kent, pages 30, 38; Selwyn Powers (Sandved & Coleman), pages 37, 42; Len Lee Rue III, page 41; Kjell B. Sandved (Sandved & Coleman), page 45.